Ctrl+Alt+Reflect

My Lens on Life, the World, and Everything in Between

SHOUVIK BANERJEE

BookLeaf Publishing

India | USA | UK

Made with ❤ on the BookLeaf Publishing Platform
www.bookleafpub.in
www.bookleafpub.com

Dedication

To all the quiet moments spent in solitude, lost in thought. These moments, often unnoticed and fleeting, have been my silent companions;guiding me, challenging me, and ultimately shaping the words on these pages. What once existed only in my mind has now found a tangible form, ready to be shared with those who seek meaning in reflection.

To the countless books that have been more than just ink on paper ;each one a window into another world, a mirror to my own thoughts, and a beacon of wisdom. And to the authors, known and unknown, whose words have sparked curiosity, stirred emotions, and influenced the way I see life, the world, and everything in between. Without their silent mentorship, this book would not have taken form.

And finally, to my partner, Indrani, and my son, Aayushmaan;thank you for your patience as I brought this book to life. Perhaps now, you're relieved (or even delighted) that it's finally complete!

Preface

This book was never meant to be a poetic endeavor,nor does it aim to potray thoughts with poetic enhancements. Instead, it began as a simple attempt to structure my reflections on a variety of subjects and share them with readers who might find a spark of novelty or resonance within them.

At its core, this collection is a articulation of thoughts—woven from life's processes, its methods, and the intricate elements of society as a whole. It questions biases, challenges existing templates, and invites introspection. It does not seek to provide answers but rather to explore the essence of our journeys.

If, by the end of this book, I leave you with a lingering question, a new perspective, or a gentle nudge toward your own reflections, then it has served its purpose. Perhaps it may even inspire you to begin penning down your own thoughts,mapping out your philosophies, your contradictions, and your unique way of seeing the world.

The words within these pages are simple. They do not claim to introduce ideas you have never encountered before. But as these poems pass through you, I hope they leave behind a quiet echo—one that lingers, stirs, and reaffirms what you believe about life and its ever-unfolding journey.

Acknowledgements

This book is a reflection of the love, support, and encouragement I have received from my family.

To **Indrani**, my partner, for your patience and quiet support through this journey. Your belief in me has meant everything.

To my son, **Aayushmaan**, for reminding me to stay curious and open to the world. Your wonder and questions inspire me every day. I hope one day, you'll find your own words and share them with the world.

To my **parents and sister**, for shaping my thoughts and values, and for encouraging me to think, reflect, and grow.

To my **father-in-law**, for his kindness, wisdom, and unwavering encouragement.

To my **friends and colleagues** , for the shared memories and the conversations.

Thank you for being a part of my journey.

1. My Life's Process

In silence, I find my path,
a gentle rhythm, unhurried by time.

Each step, a choice to explore,
to build a life of substance, not haste.

I stay with the process, steady and calm,
trusting discipline to carry me far.

Panic fades, awareness deepens
and in this stillness, I become.

Slowly, I evolve, steady all the while,
taking time, taking breath, and realizing:
when intent is strong and passion drives you,
the journey itself fulfills you.

2. Perfection – A Myth?

Perfection is a myth
a distant ideal, elusive and vague.

Is it something we can truly hold?
Or merely perceptions,
layered with subjective conceptions,
guided by what we think should be
Is the beast called Perfection

"Perfection is the end goal,"
they say,
but why have an end goal,
my question lay

Perfection binds you,
Perfection limits you ,
Perfection stifles you,
and before long,
it suffocates you .

Lean towards the journey instead—
a journey of progress,
a journey of improvement,
A journey of reflection and eventually,
A journey of evolution.

This journey has no end,
it fuels your creativity,
it fulfills you ,
it builds you, And
it makes you whole

And finally,
you feel you've arrived,
and you become,
yourself.

And when that happens,
The journey has fulfilled
It's promise
And it's purpose

3. Solitude

Solitude for me is not emptiness,
Solitude for me is not nothingness.
It's space that liberates,
Where thoughts flow freely,
Where my deepest aspirations unravel.

I feel my heartbeat,
I feel the warmth of my breath
I am here, alive, aware.
That's how my space feels,
That's how my world is.

I love walking by silent shores,
Listening to my own voice, my whispers.

It's the blue ocean, the endless sky,
And the space between them
That completes me.
My solitude liberates,

My solitude defines,
My solitude helps me become who I am.

4. The Gift of Pause

Are you in a hurry?
A hurry to live,
A hurry to feel,
A hurry to gather the scattered pieces of your mind?

Perhaps, all you need is a pause.
A quiet pause to reflect,
To gaze within,
To study the crossroads where life gently nudges you.

For if we rush, we lose
The beauty of the unfolding journey,
The space to grow,
The wisdom to mature,
The courage to evolve.

And, most of all,
We lose our chance to truly live.

5. The Forgotten Essence of Being

I ponder, therefore I exist.
I speak, and I feel alive.
I write, to keep my spirit breathing,
To let my expressions thrive.

But what are we, if not our ability to act?
What holds us back
What binds our sails?

Which race do we run,
When we all finish at the same Mark,
Where ambition shadows passion,
Matter outweighs meaning,
And opinion drowns depth?
Where information replaces wisdom,
And we lose ourselves in the rush?

Why don't we sit with ourselves and talk,
Hear what we truly feel?

Why don't we become our closest friends?
In that quiet union, we find a way
The way to discovery,
The way to self-awareness,
The way to becoming whole.

6. The Tranquility within Me

Embrace life's joys,
They are here to uplift you,
Embrace life's challenges,
They are here to strengthen you.
Embrace each moment,
For it carries lessons untold,
Embrace the unknown,
For its where your courage unfolds.
Embrace yourself fully,
Both your shadow and light,
For it's in self-acceptance,
That your soul takes flight.
When you honor your flaws,
And cherish your grace,
You'll find a calmness,
A serene inner space.
No need to battle,
No need to pretend,
In loving yourself,

True peace begins to transcend.
It's in the stillness within,
Where harmony resides,
A gentle, quiet knowing,
That no storm can divide.

7. A Life well Embraced

What follows a bright, sunny day is the calm and
antiquity of night.
What follows scorching heat are the mesmerizing
droplets of rain.
What follows days of sorrow are moments of fulfillment
and light.

Life moves in circles; you end where you begin.
Embrace all that comes your way, for it is the whole that
defines you within.

What would you be, my friend, without your dash of
flaws?
Who would recognize you, if not for the gift of
vulnerability?
How would you grow, if life didn't test you with trials
and laws?

Amalgamate, embrace life's every experience
For it's all part of a plan that completes you to the core.

It's what makes you whole; it's who you are.

12

8. My Regrets Complete me

I don't keep regrets,
I embrace them.
I don't dwell on my shortcomings
They complete me.

When I look within,
I see vulnerabilities,
I see insecurities,
Vices nestled beside virtues
Some in small measure,
Others in abundance.

Yet I gather them all,
As night gathers the light of dawn.
For in acceptance blooms renewal,
And in renewal, the seeds of progress.

How else to banish the shadows?
How else to cross the barren droughts?
If not by honoring

The chaos within.

This is my source of peace,
A stillness deep and true:
To know the dark, the light,
And every shade between
Is not just part of me,
In fact, it is me.

9. The Quiet Ascent of Evolution

Evolution isn't a choice
it's the pulse within our veins,
the whisper in the wind,
the ember in the chains.

We break, we bend, we rise, we fall,
yet through it all, we heed the call.

Winds will shift, rivers bend,
moons will wane, and nights will end.
Leaves will fall, tides will rise,
time will dance before our eyes
yet change remains.

To acknowledge, to accept ,is the real leap
Don't resist, don't fight, flow with the change,
and you'll find ,
peace within.

You quiet the echoes,
soften the tide,
settle your demons,
And quiet the storms , as serenity takes root,
Deep inside

Evolution is not just change
it's when change becomes you.
It's when you dissolve into the ever-turning tide,
And take up the liberating ride .

Thats when you emerge ,
From shadows of your own self,
Thats when you become - The change

10. Between Silence and Sirens

The city is bustling
With people, hope, aspirations, and dreams.
Its vibrancy hums,
In the blare of horns, the rush of wheels,
And endless streams of traffic weaving through concrete
veins.

The city never sleeps,
It hustles, relentless,
A vortex of motion and commotion.

Yet, my friend,
Why do you still search for yourself?
Why does your gaze seem distant,
Your smile, a fleeting shadow?

The city, with all its vigor,
With its concrete towers and glittering lights,
Still falls short of what you seek.

It's a place where dreams come true,
Where innovation burns bright,
Where spirits pulse with life —
And yet, you linger, searching for answers.

Perhaps the city fulfills some dreams,
But leaves others to wander
On an endless journey,
A quiet quest,
To find what's missing within.

11. The Land of Many Contradictions

We sit side by side, screens aglow,
Yet strangers in cubicles row by row.
We click and connect across distant lands,
But seldom shake the closest hands.

We chase the sky with tireless feet,
Yet seek a rhythm, calm and sweet.
Craving balance, we toil and strive,
A delicate dance, just staying alive.

We measure worth in outputs, clear,
Yet cherish the process, slow and sincere.
The goal in sight, the steps we trace
Every detail, a measured grace.

We love our quiet, the peace we find,
Yet yearn for family close behind.
In solitude's lap, our hearts may roam,
But love brings us back, it feels like home.

We scroll through worlds with restless eyes,
But pause for stories that mesmerize.
A movie's frame, our minds hold tight,
Brief escapes from endless bytes.

We count our money, our minutes too,
Both precious, both fleeting, both askew.
Our passions flare, interests swell,
Yet leisure sparks debates that swell.

Strangers grow into friends with time,
Conversations twist, then start to rhyme.
Sadness may linger, but hope lights the way,
Happiness fleeting, we seize each day.

Such is my country, layered and deep,
A land of contradictions we gently keep.
Of passion, of life, of thoughts that collide
A beautiful paradox where we all reside.

12. The Box we forgot to Open

We execute, we drive, we do
The world rewards the busy crew.

But in this rush, what slips away?
The space to think, to carve away.

Ideas weaken, creativity wanes,
And mediocrity tightens its chains.
We craft machines to obey and perform,
Yet lose the courage to challenge the norm.

For progress isn't in speed alone,
Nor in the seeds efficiency has sown.
Excellence thrives where thoughts collide,
Where boldness reigns, and dreams reside.

Society cannot leap ahead
On paths of old, forever tread.
Evolution demands a step aside,

A pause, a look at where we reside.

It calls for minds that dare to stray,
To question, "Where do we go from here today?"
Rethinking isn't just a choice,
It's the essence of a forward voice.

Let us not mistake movement for growth,
Nor profits for purpose—let's hold them both.
To open the box is to embrace the unknown,
To let the seeds of tomorrow be sown.

For evolution is the trickiest game,
But without it, all we build is the same.
Let's quiet the noise, let thought ignite,
And guide this world towards its next great light.

13. Intrigue and Progress

Why don't we question enough?
Why don't we harbor doubts?
Why do we seem so secure?
Where is the intrigue?
Sometimes, all we need is

A little doubt,
A little vulnerability,
A touch of madness,
And a hint of jeopardy.

To break the mold,
To shatter the template,
To dismantle the framework,
And open the box.
What, after all, leads to progress,
If not questions, doubts,
And a new process?
Chase your doubts, my friend,
For you are doing yourself a favor.

The same doubts will shape your future character.
Pursue them, nurture them, grow them,
For the fruits they bear shall give you answers,

And that, my friend, will be your progress.
You will become an advancer.

Why don't we question enough?
Why don't we harbor doubts...

14. Fading of ideologies

We live in a world where ideologies fade,
Where lives dissolve into bits and bytes.
Transactions now take center stage
In work, in love, in fleeting nights.

What we see, what we seek,
Is measured, tactical, and planned.

But what we miss
Is the vast, uncharted horizon.
We miss the compass of values
The spark that drives us,
The flame that inspires us,
The wonder that once ignited our days.

We no longer ask why our hearts beat,
Instead, we ask:
What do I gain?
Where's the profit?
What's the yield of this moment's trade?

Our lives unfold as profit and loss ledgers,
Our emotions ride the waves of the markets.
Give and take becomes our currency,
But the soul starves in this exchange.

In the noise of negotiations,
We forget the art of nurturing bonds,
The quiet joy of solitude,
The tranquil grace of nothingness,
The beauty of an unclaimed moment.

We barter our peace for productivity,
And lose ourselves in the chase.

Amidst the ticking clocks and calculated gains,
What we truly miss
Is ourselves.

15. In the Company of Virtues

Humility and Confidence met one day,
Sipping tea on a bright, sunny display.
Exchanging pleasantries, their voices light,
Debating their paths in the soft, fading light.

I like to stay grounded,' said Humility,
'While I may take the occasional flight,' gestured
Confidence.
'I am present in people's behavior, their relations, and
their demeanor,' suggested Humility.
'Well, I am in their attitude, their mind, and their
actions,' queried Confidence.
'I may not guarantee success, but I ensure people can
handle success,' said Humility.
'On the contrary, I assist in success,' quietly suggested
Confidence.
'What are we, then, to people?'
Popped a question in their conversation.

'Are we different or the same?
Are we essential or banal?
Are we present, or are we the mind's gestation?
What are we, dear friend?'
'Well, we complement each other,' suggested Confidence,
And he continued,
'While my necessity precedes success, your necessity
succeeds it.
While I reside in tactical faculties, you are in hearts and
minds.
While my presence grows stronger with time, your
presence helps me grow.'

So, not so different after all,
'But birds of the same feather,' commented Humility,
As they walked into the sunset,
To meet another day,
And debate on their way.

16. Books

These lovely collections of words,
In pages so neatly bound,
Have been my source of inspiration,
And joy, unmeasured, unbound.
Some reveal the whispers of history,
While others reflect society's core,
Some unveil maps and geographies,
Or lead to memories we adore.

Each one, a steadfast companion,
Each, a unique tale to tell,
Immersed in their vivid worlds,
I've journeyed where legends dwell.

Remarkable events come alive,
Through stories that endlessly thrive.
It's truly a wonder how books ignite,
Bringing knowledge and wonder to light.
I wouldn't be a fraction of who I am,
Or think the thoughts I have today,

Without the books that grace my shelves,
My treasure, my guide, in every way.

17. Embracing cracks of Imperfection

We smooth the edges, paint the cracks,
Chasing dreams of flawless tracks.
Yet in the lines that twist and break,
Lies the path we're meant to take.

A blemish here, a scar so slight,
Marks of battles lost in light.
Yet aren't we shaped by what's unplanned?
By trembling heart and trembling hand?

Imperfection stirs the mind awake,
A hunger born of each mistake.
It pulls us closer, makes us see,
The boundless depth of all we'll be.

It softens words, it melts the space,
Where judgment fades and love takes place.
For when we drop the need to hide,
We stand as truth, not polished pride.

A hand that falters, yet holds tight,
A voice unsure, yet speaks what's right
These quiet flaws, so gently spun,
Are how we love, how trust is won.

So wear your scars, let go of pride,
Let flaws be doors, not walls to hide.
For all we are, and all we seek,
Is woven through the cracks we keep.

18. Rendezvous with the my younger self

Today, I undertake a rendezvous
with my younger self.
I talk to him about life,
sharing perspectives ;Agreeing on some,
while many remain in strife.

We collaborate on thoughts,
discuss relations,
And as we speak, we realize—
we're still where we were,
only the lenses have changed,
and the world around us.

The substance remains the same;
similar are the conflicts,
but our reactions now differ
to the circumstances.

Is it maturity? Is it evolution?

I don't know.
I may not want to know.

What matters is that we are different,
yet somehow, always the same
at our core,
we remain unbroken,
still learning, still becoming.

19. Beyond Change , Begins Transformation

I never seek to change,
For change feels fleeting,
An excuse wrapped in reason,
A justification seeking purpose

Seldom does change
Stem from true interest,
Seldom does it stay,
Seldom does it create you.

But they say,
"Change is permanent,
Change is necessary"

I say,
I may not agree, my friend.

What I seek instead
Is transformation.

Transformation inspires.
Transformation is internal,
Transformation is personal,
And it is permanent.

It builds character,
Becomes a steadfast ally,
A quiet force reshaping life.

While change is tactical,
Transformation is visionary.

So, my friend,
Look for transformation,
And you will find yourself building
Creating, growing,
Far beyond the reach of change.
Are you now ready to Change or Perhaps
Transform?

20. Is Emptiness truly empty ?

I find magic in emptiness,
I find magic in solace.
There's an ethereal beauty in nature
the ocean, the sky,
and just me.

The world and its desires drift far away,
my ambitions fade,
my quest for wealth dissolves.
What matters in that moment
is the stillness offered,
the chance to meet myself,
to discover who I am.

I tell nature, I am, after all,
a part of you,
and in this emptiness,
I become you.

Is that what emptiness means
coming closer to your roots?

21. Hope

I look forward to the change of seasons ,
Spring , Summer , Monsoon and Winter
It's nature's way of keeping us engaged through its
banter ,

I look forward to each day ,
The hustle filled Monday through Thursday,
And thanking God for Friday,
It presents new hope and Zeist ensuring our moods don't
turn grey

I look forward to meeting new people ,
From acquaintances at work to strangers searching their
way ,
From long lost friends to new peers , all of them, add
their bit to life
And make it a jovial liveable day

What would be life , if I don't look forward,
How would I feel , if each day does not bring hope ,

Hope of excitement, Hope of enlightenment, Hope of
knowledge

Look forward, my friend,
That's life way of keeping us interested and curious,

What do you look forward to ?

www.ingramcontent.com/pod-product-compliance
Lightning Source LLC
Chambersburg PA
CBHW061725130726
47996CB00006B/2498